I0444496

# Seven Hills

## By Calvin Marshall

Copyright © 2018 Calvin Clarence Marshall

All rights reserved.

ISBN: 1986937666
ISBN-13: 9781986937665

"I bet if the world was black & white

I believe people will still see color in transparent places."

## -Calvin Marshall

# BlackonBlackRhyme

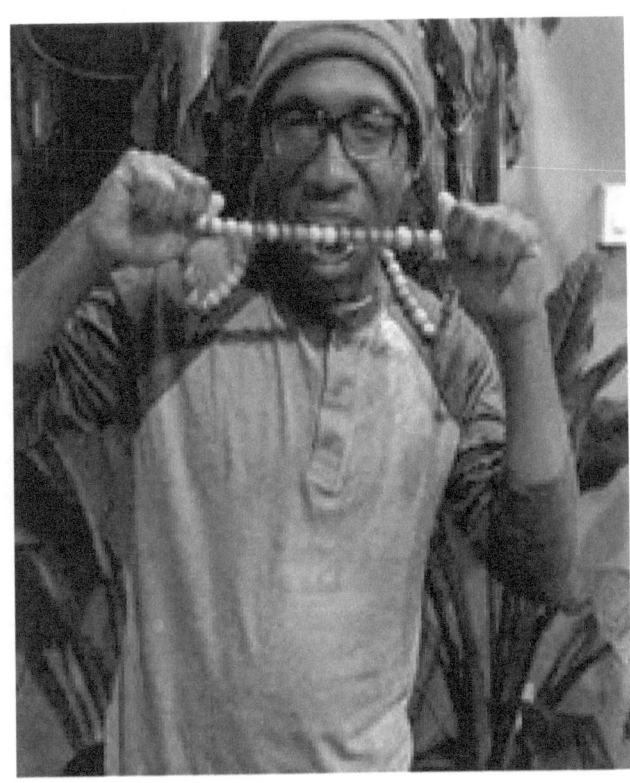

# Unfaithful News

Just praying to a God, that I don't believe in

If I am being faithful tell me why she creeping…?

Broken tears started leaking

Barely whole

She broke away from us


Wonder why dishonesty is in my veins

Cause I got broken and she got brand new

I guess this the words …Unfaithful News


I am black

But I turn blue

What a man supposed

To accomplish

When the whole reason

Why I was breathing

Was you....


Holidays

Were the worst

She sent the letters I refuse to read

Pack her stuff now she only comes to pass me by

Kisses were air because high fives were a cringe

Babe I change I even accept your infidelity

Maybe try polyamory

Listening to En Vogue

"What's it, going to be...?"

We have the right to lose control...

I can understand this

# Seven Hills

Broken with edgy heart

She got back to love making baby

We have to unpack our bags

I will drive to your destination

With no more reason to lose my patience

Out our own issues

Just call my phone I am only a minute away

However, I see through the window

She is happily engage

Now I realize

I am missing you

Calvin Marshall

# *See what you think*

I stole I shouldn't

Nevertheless, I know I could

Snatching purses

Buying new shirts

Matching jeans

I will be cute

You will see

This time everybody will notice me

# Seven Hills

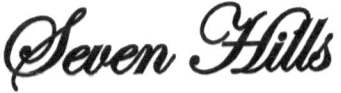

popular group of friends

That I will lead

Funny fingers laughing

Names

I will be cool

Like a breeze

So let me be!


Corner store up the street

I run in no mask

Baseball cap flip back

Clerk say

how may I help you sir

While Sir you getting jack

I will be rich so I will pay you back

Sirens in the distance blue got me hesitating

Wait...

It is too late to turn back

School tomorrow

I have to look fly


Snatch those twenties

those nickels too

I duck and dodge until I am out of sight

Notice this truth is a horrible sight

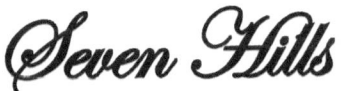

Too cool for too much school

So now, I choose dropout to steal

To be cool....

Calvin Marshall

# Blind

If you can't see

It happening

That is okay

Closed minds cannot relate

You hear those sirens in the distance blue

White T-shirt

Colored holes

Bullets

Came through


Those streets

We either predator or prey

Be eaten or lay

It is crazy

# Seven Hills

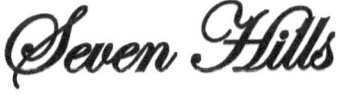

However, best learn this way


Question

Why should we bury our sons or daughters?

Before our parents die

Knowing that! Only

Gets windows shattered and chest to floor

Heads down

Please no peek holes

Something lurking outside

New York City

**Harlem** nights or **Chicago** winters

**Section 8** or **Manhattan**

Living nice or keep **struggle alive**

If I knew back than would I even care?

I see Pastors take

Prostitutes become millionaires

Mo' money, Mo' problems

With a barrel of a hole pointed my direction

# Seven Hills

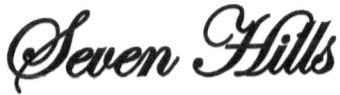

R.I.P

Like maybe, it is a better destination

Afterlife we could not see

Then I realize

Even ghouls and ghost

**Have Hell**

**Cold world**

**Los Angeles**

So many stories told

Therefore, man will never ride

So centered on maybes we live our lives

Like a pillow we sleep


Dreaming on better lives

Would you be ready to go?

If only he gave us a choice to know

I hate the fact Tallahassee, Florida

Crimes high

I sneak outside like mama

Told me not to go outside


But Mama

I must witness reality

For even Picasso painted tragedy

Yes, I see now

# Seven Hills

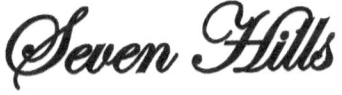

## Outsmokin

Baby I could not imagine my life with you

You constant think of my flaws

When I say yours beautiful


The seed we planted will grow

Knowing the toxic environment

Face the dilemmas

Yea...I know

Choose the outside window

But if I leave you as a single mom

I will be deadbeat father

Kids will be curious

From the words he heard and pictures of us

School uniforms

Kissing and carrying on

Knowing damn well

We were wrong


I cried tears and I know you

salty about

However, babe...!

Damn that you got my babe

Better, handle that

I know the exact moment you burst I felt that

# Seven Hills

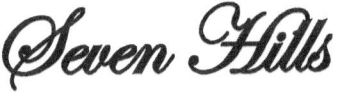

So you not leaving this child without a father

Just understand

But babe...!?!?!


I gave you this womb now it's

Too much for you

Stand in this emergency room

Wait for your baby girl

See time is a bitch

Child support makes me laugh

I do not want to be ghetto in this hospital

However I would whoop that Ass


I lick your kids

Now you will not see them come

Like a fire with no heat

Why you trying to stay warm


All I am saying take this seed

Wonder what I did before made you see

Now you confuse because babe is not baby

However, lately, you create space

So what you gone choose....


I conjure remedies of lies

Floating in my head to leave

Blending feelings and heartfelt words bleed

I tried to be honest hopefully

She would not see

That she was not my main

Just a side an open leg and a piece

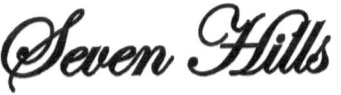

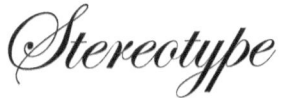

I bet if the world was black & white

People will still see color in transparent places

They box us in by the colors of our skin

**Stereotype**

That person could not create that

However, refrain to congregate to praise efforts

Instead, you oppose the fact

Who created it?

... Like

Touch-tone phone by a Black Men


**Stereotype**


He is Asian and all those look alike

They must be fish heads that are scientist

Leading the world in this Market


**Stereotype**


I should hate this Man

Who created stoplights?

Garrett Morgan that was a dick move

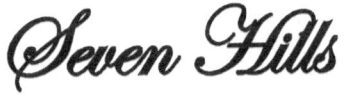

## Stereotype

Charles drew organized

The first blood bank in the U.S

Nevertheless, he couldn't be Black


## Stereotype

This will not be culture against culture

We have our own kind

Who pollutes the generational?


That every black child

Need to be a rapper or an athletic

Figure

Now that will not be fact

Give me education or give me death


Got guys who don't want

Gold diggers

But throw stacks

Plus women don't want to be sex symbols

But use those bodies for those stacks

How ironic is that...

Now maybe

That is total fact

Not a


**Stereotype**

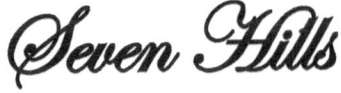

Every Hispanic

Must be an illegal immigrant

**Stereotype**

Every white person is a racist

**Stereotype**

Willis Johnson

Created that rotary egg beater

Who wouldn't want to eat that?

## Stereotype

I remember we could not record

A thing now that is whack

Who created this?

Was Benjamin Thornton

He Asian not black


## Stereotype

That every other culture appropriate

Music from black people

I mean this can't be acknowledge truthfully

# Seven Hills

We got some weak songs too


**"Sweet Home Alabama"**

That was a mega hit

Plus an icon of mines too

He was a Caucasian dude


Oh let's not stereotype this one either

Those women are gay if they look more masculine

Okay I admit that one I'm a little confuse

So before, I finish look around the room

Every person in this bitch is broke

See!

**I just stereotype you**

# Too Fast

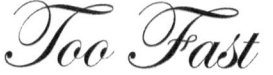

I once drove too fast

Clearly for laughs

Even beside my

Future

Leaving the past

No reference to my

Gas

Press pedal

I pass

# Seven Hills

Life I gain

Years I strain


For the time is essence

With thunder came that

Rain


Careful I drove for now years slowed

The year is 2020

I am very old

Cause live freely

Now pain is food

Therefore, I starve the stomach and life is crude

For I drove right pass

Every chance I had

Long enough for day dreams and

Money piles


She was once in a moment of joy

That dance move groove

Closer then love tomorrow the door

Therefore, I drove again for time is essence

For no man I leave behind

Piss poor...

# Seven Hills

## Flower sunken place

Want you be a mine?

No need to be unsatisfied,

I be the rock the boat kind,

No rush the flow kind,

You see. Gentlemen I be,

Money I keep,

No sleep till I see,

The morning face of your beauty

However, forget all that cause

Want you be mine?

hmm...


Sure, you are fine

Mi mind though

Wonders more ponders more

Could he truly be mi kind?




The Kind to worship

The grounds I walk

Want to be around just for talks

Skinny-dipping…birth date suits

# Seven Hills

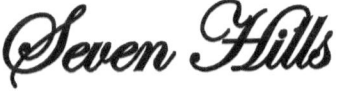

Summer time cruises I would say atlest two


Would he pick mi a'gain now?

That he can see that

I am most picky….choosy…

At time even a bit snoody

Mi mind wonders more

Mi mind ponders more


I kinder understand

but let us see

Would you want it to be open

or a little discreet?

Do not kid the kid

with complacent wonders

Why dream with boundless hopes


When I am hoping to be your G.O.A.T

Your quench your thirst kind

Open doors for you

Play with the newborn and care for you

Sip you taste you be amazing for the camera view

Kind


But I always wonder am I beyond my years

Treating you better than my peers

Peeling the orange peel for you

Kinder being mean and ignoring your calls

Just to set the record straight though

# Seven Hills

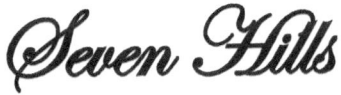

We both understood


What is real and what's fake

Stop with the dialogue

Enough with the sexual tension

Just wanted to know

Would you mind to be my kind?


Boy you want to choose to chase me

But if I let you in

You could not never replace thee

I got a PHD in natural body turning heads

And leaving trails of thirsty dudes in my wake

Therefore, if you ponder more maybe you mine in

another realm of possibilities


Until I focus my time of yoga bends

Stretching pass your rules I stand by myself

If you a toll allow me to turn the doorknob to be

by myself cause, my mind wonders

More ponders more

Do I need to reveal anymore?

# Seven Hills

## Dreadful Days

Questions remain from the struggle I strain

Should love be deceit?

Cracking the dame, we suppose to remain

Solid like an open sparrow


Eating mother earth 4 seasons

I mean four reasons to scatter ones alchemy

That adoring foot step in the sand dunes we play

Fitting inbox boxes of conflicts would have evil let

it stay


Forrest into the mountain fray

Deep in valleys lower then oceans floors

Kisses are bittersweet like grapefruit beats

Sounds from echo keeps moving motions

Beneath naked freak


Thoughts like an empty space

Ripping the final breath

Out of lungs away

Should I die without you?


Couldn't the scent of poison

Be the taste I knew you for?

Ticking tocking until the tick stop clocking

# Seven Hills

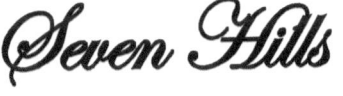

And moments likes these fade


I surrounded her like roses on a casket

Like instrument notes at Famu Set

Like lying from every

Word possible in the alphabet

I stay cold

Weaklings unfold

The wolves come to feast


Run little puppy because the table isn't enough for

us all

That animal raging

For innocence while people walk astray

Threading blood on palms faces

Praying God come through the Heaven gates

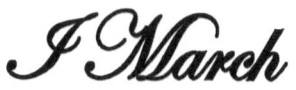

I March now


Mother can't you see?


I am marching to be free


The police bring cubs to beat


But no, no, no

# Seven Hills

They cannot see

Mother!

Mother!

Can I march with?

My fellow men and fellow child

This is Independence Day

Can't you see?

I no longer can stand to watch

This country chain our freedom

I'm gonna March to be

Free

Mother and fathers let go

Of your son and daughters

Let them march with me

We marching to be FREE!

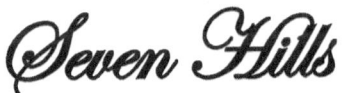

## Dear Mama

I know it is hard I see the pain

I know you do the 24/7 jobs

To make hot plates on tables

Evicted cause the property owner will not see the

struggle

You are my guardian over all


Love how you cook my fav Mac and Cheese

Fighting for my needs because you know I'll grow

Than the ghetto I see

I know the blessings come

However, ill repay you

With the love you always shown

Dreaming about fame to show my mom I get that

big house for her

To give an inch to the mile you walk for five kids

No worries now sleep tight I hold it down tonight

love you

Dear Mama

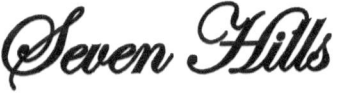

## Ghettoes

I took one-way ticket to escape

A mark of death hairy trigger paranoid of

Niggers

Ghetto bastards I hate this life

On warfare only time cops help

Cell silence on hell blocks


Can't sleep feared of graveyard shift

Time ticking a sentence I could not repent

Preachers am not save they're

Sticking hands in cookie jars

Offering paradise

When they judge lies of decent living


I shell tears homies go blind

From the other side

God choose favorites

When devil kill lives

Careful steps

As I took a bag of chains

Reaping the sour fruits

From Adam and Eve

Trees better yet weed

# Seven Hills

## Lil Homie

Lil Homie

Wanted to be a leader

Kept up on the square was hit but a hollow point

unknown when the other homies heard they laugh

now... Who is the dummy?

When the generation getting played

...now I'm confessing


No teachers in the lessons

Only a besties spreading drugs and disease

lil homie  being another kid in the crude streets

just lost his way now his mother

Watch the news with sorrowful reviews


Tamika was not educated

On the other hand, so she thought

# Seven Hills

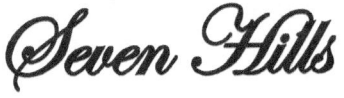

Temptation pulled the wool over her thoughts

Being consume of the

Fast life met a boy she call hubby

Posting blogs and Instagram pictures

So one night was not

a fairytale

Just a misunderstanding

Tamika was shot

Multiplied by 10 times 5

Just being herself


Being seen with a friend

In addition, he lost his nerve

Being buried by anger

And hairy trigger fingers

Now she played to rest

May she R.I.P

Nevertheless, the story continues

Follow the leader

I see you

When you get there

Lil Homie


Three lil homies was friends

Up until the time they were

Robbing a convenience store

Over on 5th Ave in Harlem

Knowing one patrol at night

Therefore, it should be an ease

Striding cross the street creeping

# Seven Hills

Into the front door


Yelling down motherfucker

Give me the cash

lil homie had the door

The other in the middle, one at the counter


The scene was lockdown..

Until a bright light blind the

Last sight 12 shots nobody crawl out

Little homies got a lesson hard learn

We live by the lesson we choose to learn

The define reality

Strings its pain into our everyday lives

"**We** either **Stand or** fall **for everything**"

## Stay Float

The fact that we see the person

Whom you will gave the world too

Only spite in your face because

The only time she needs you


Is to blind the fact you were

Ever needed

Because the guy she want

Is not the one you thought you created?

It is a profile pic on the phone

In her heart, this is bullshit

# Seven Hills

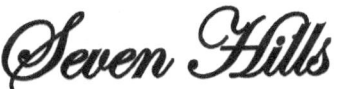

Still you believe ...poetry


Would you take a bow?

With a broken arrow

I know I must leave

But how are you so hallow


I wanted chances too many chances

Run after you onto of

Shadows behind the screen

You so selfish I cannot stand your ass

Would you remember who help you or take the

wheel?

You say time heals you

But you never seen

The shadow behind the screen

I hate you for that pain pills

I overdose again

would you stop being petty

Knowing I love

You

But you never seen

# Seven Hills

The shadow behind the screen

## Magic

I got a piece of that magic

I make it appear like a hat with a habit

Then I disappear in the alley like an addict

Life no fairytale it's clear tragic

Living three minutes

Gone in mere, mere, seconds

Can anybody, somebody, tell me what happen?

Brenda got a baby

Now she want her BD on the TL

But  he say maybe

See? Shit so crazy

But she reach way down

in the mix of the bullshit

And pull some out in her palms

You see.

# Seven Hills

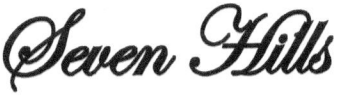

Brenda got a piece of that magic

She make it appear like a hat with a habit

Then she disappear in the alley like an addict


Life no fairytale

It is clear tragic

Living three minutes

Gone in mere, mere, mere seconds

Can anybody, somebody, tell me what happen?


Bill Captain Pop, Pill popper

Captain Pop ,Pill Popper

Captain Pop, Pill Popper

Off in the cut, pill dropper

Bill got a problem

He don't want anybody to see

So he wait for his wife to leave

And hide behind closed doors

He do it early in the morning

And in the mist of the night

You see?


Bill got a piece of that magic

He make it appear like a hat with a habit

Then he disappear like an addict in an alley

Life no fairytale its clear tragic

Living three minutes

Gone mere, mere, seconds

Can anybody, somebody, tell me what happen?

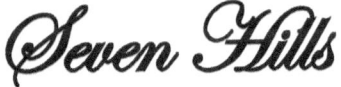

And that's call Magic


But hold on wait...


Lets' go two for two

Michael and Mary

Mary the aggressor

**Michael the lesser**

Michael tried to bless her

But Mary was a bad bitch!

She had that magazine body

I even tried to get at her

But Michael love her

Through & through

He was true & true


Until one night, he came home early just to

surprise her

Went up those stairs

That sound he heard

Was so profound?

What did he see?

Another dude was beating Mary down

He run right back down stairs reach deep into that

kitchen cabinet

# Seven Hills

Pull some out that was tragic

Pull some out that was magic

Because he had a little bit of that magic

He had a little bit of that tragic

And click click boom

Michael & Mary

Came down stairs

And she smile

She smile…

Because she use the money from Michael death

For his life insurance policy

To become a badder bitch!

Paid in full….

## FAREWELL

Thank you, so much! I have so much admiration for whomever is reading "Flowers in a Stream." I wanted to say I love you and wish you all the best in this world. Also, thank you for all the support into this last book.

**"BUT YOU DON'T HEAR ME THOUGH."**

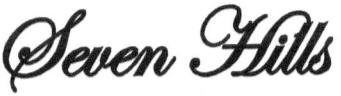

## Contact information

For inquires about owning the other copies

**AMAZON:**

**Soul Food Ed.1    ISBN: 1539108449**

**All Summers Ed.2   ISBN:  1540526925**

**Flowers in a Stream Ed.3 ISBN: 1986830071**

**Booking Outspoken!!!!**

**Contact Email: calvin.marshall29@gmail.com**

**Please continue to the next page for reflecting**

# Calvin Marshall

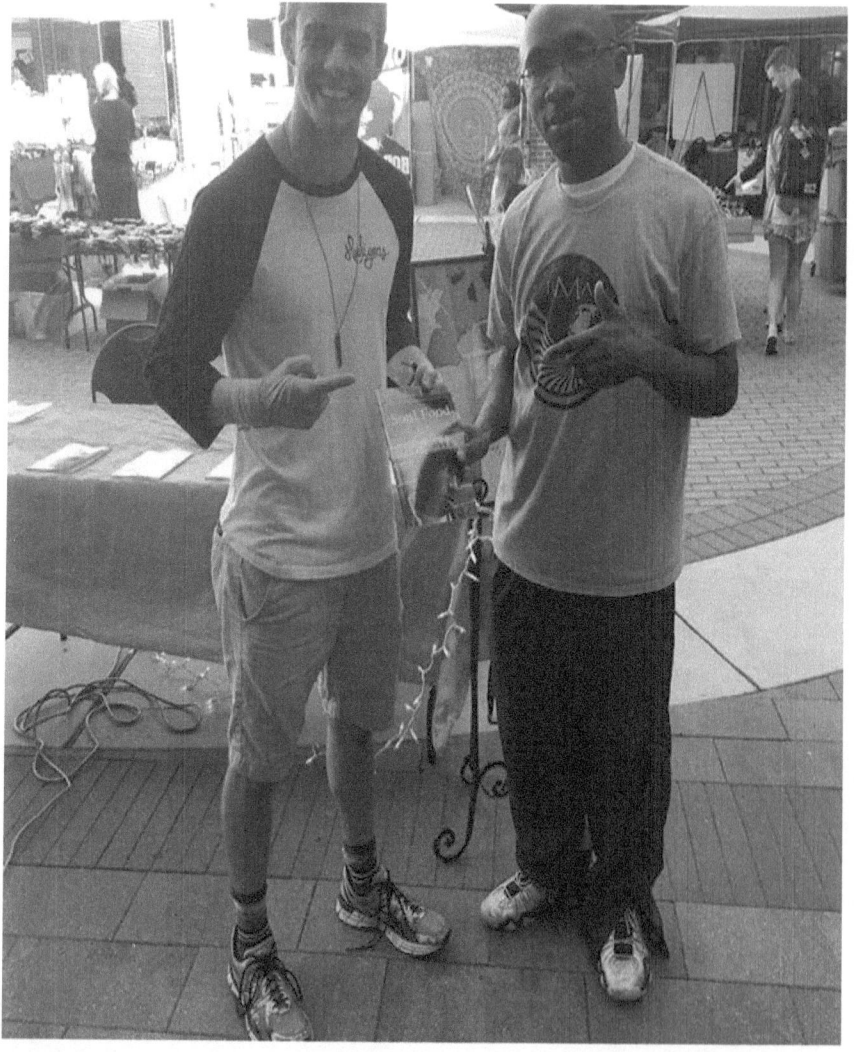

# Seven Hills

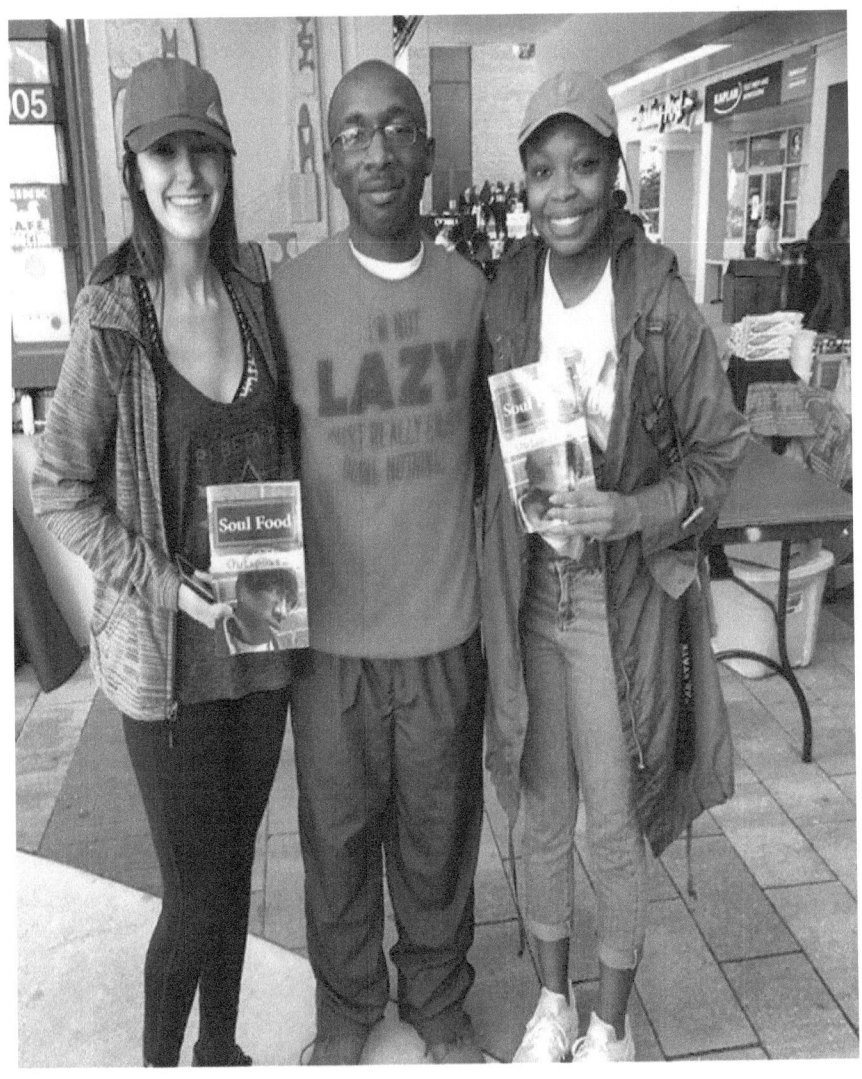

Calvin Marshall

64

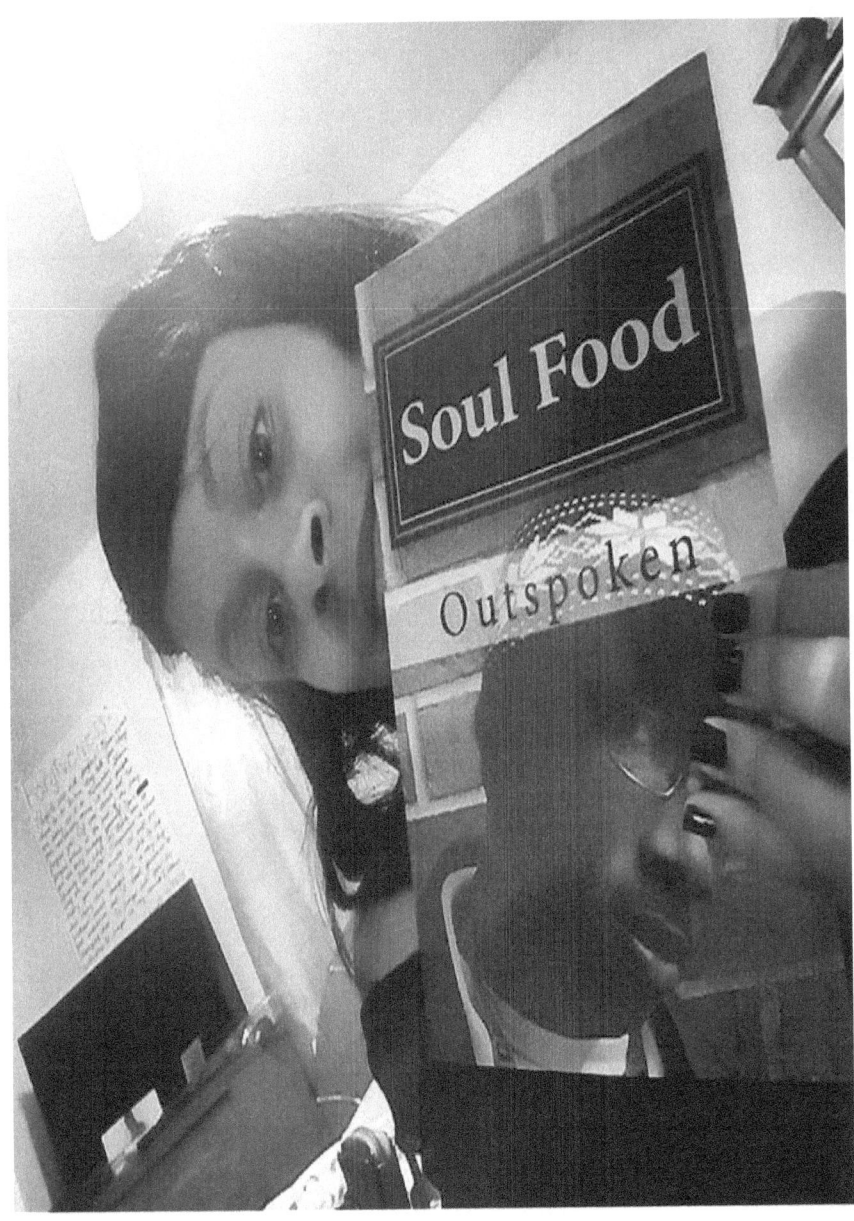

# Calvin Marshall

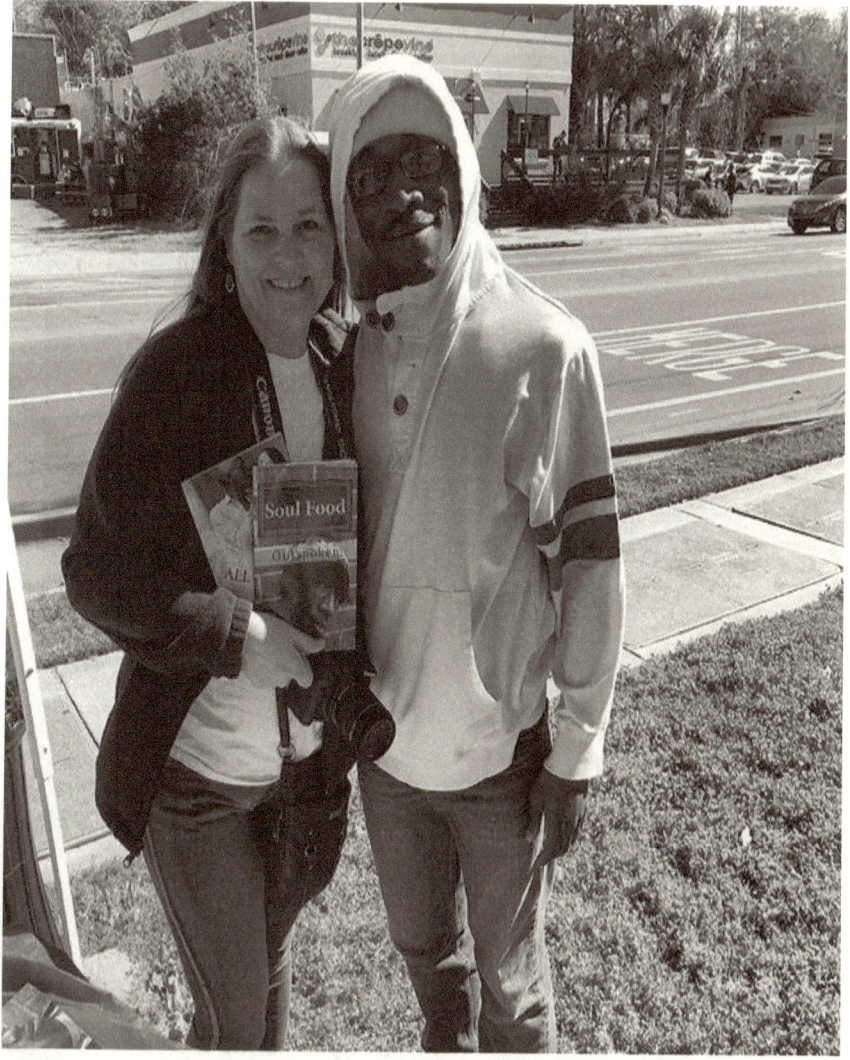

# Seven Hills

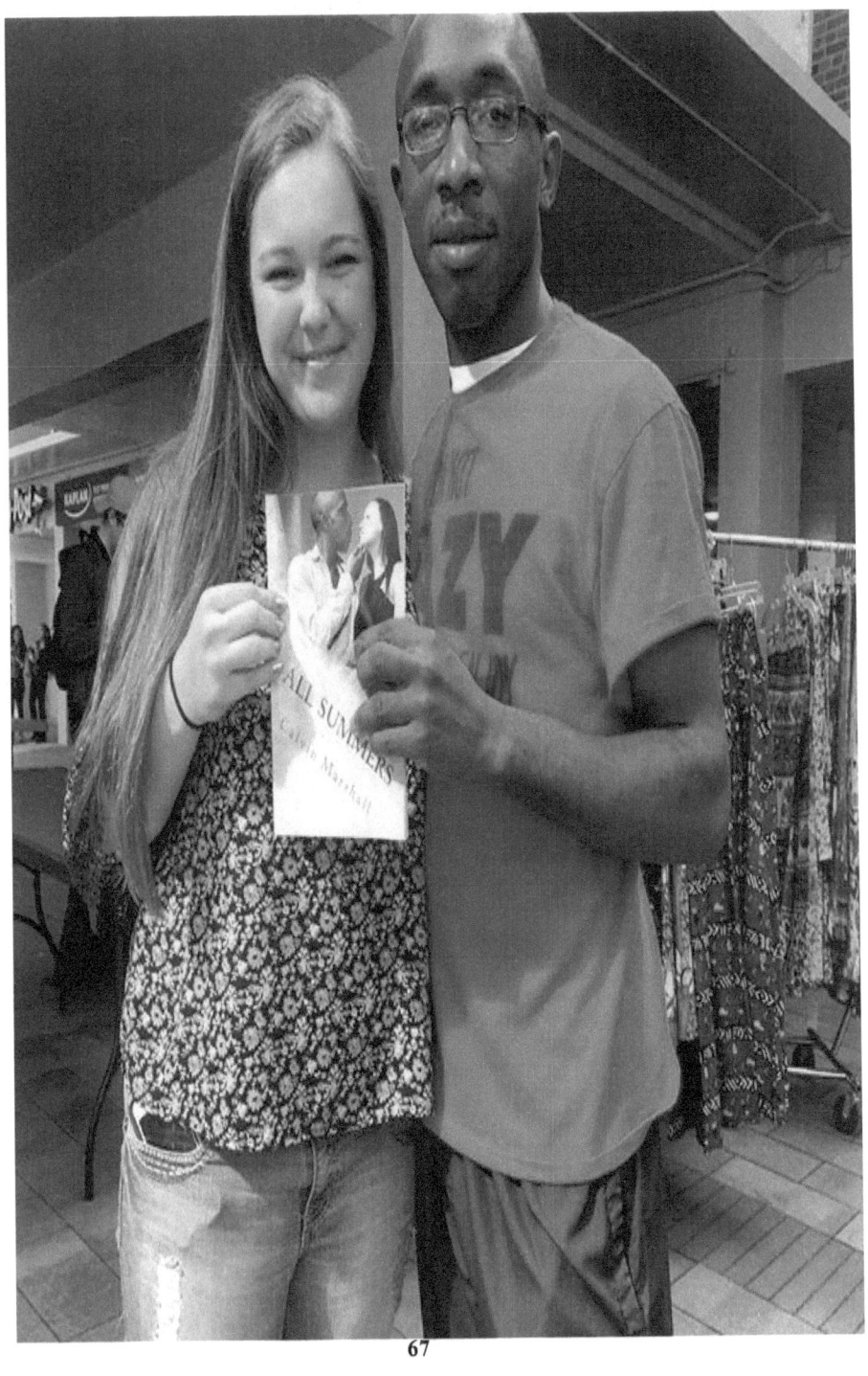

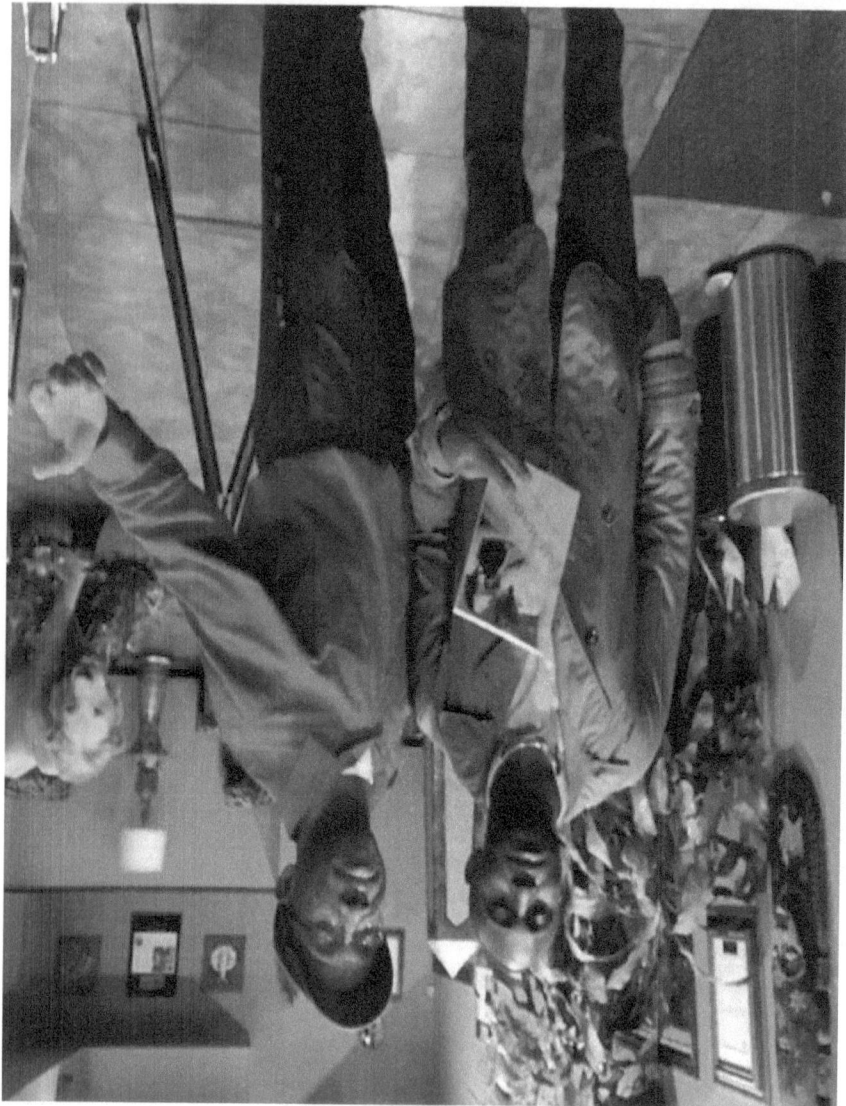

Calvin Marshall

www.ingramcontent.com/pod-product-compliance
Lightning Source LLC
Chambersburg PA
CBHW031542210526
45464CB00003B/1104